8 contemporary pie es for Ol
8 zeitgenössische Stücke für ORGEL

UNBEATEN TRACKS

Edited by John Scott

page	CONTENTS	
6	Huw Watkins	*Fanfare*
10	Diana Burrell	*Fragment I*
12		*Fragment II*
14	Roxanna Panufnik	*Bridal Train*
18	David Matthews	*Invocation*
20	Errollyn Wallen	*Tiger*
26	Graham Fitkin	*Wedding*
34	Judith Bingham	*St. Bride, assisted by angels*
41	David Bedford	*Carillon*

Unbeaten Tracks (organ) was commissioned by
The Royal College of Organists with funds also made available by
The Britten–Pears Foundation and the Kenneth Leighton Trust

© 2001 by Faber Music Ltd
First published in 2001 by Faber Music Ltd
3 Queen Square London WC1N 3AU
Cover by Økvik Design
Music processed by MusicSet 2000
German translation by Dorothee Göbel
Printed in England by Caligraving Ltd
All rights reserved

ISBN 0-571-51977-6

To buy Faber Music publications or to find out about the
full range of titles available please contact your local music
retailer or Faber Music sales enquiries:

Faber Music Ltd, Burnt Mill, Elizabeth Way, Harlow CM20 2HX
Tel: +44 (0)1279 82 89 82   Fax: +44 (0)1279 82 89 83
sales@fabermusic.com   www.fabermusic.com

THE ROYAL COLLEGE OF ORGANISTS

FABER *ff* MUSIC

PREFACE

I am delighted to have been involved in this collaboration between Faber and The Royal College of Organists to produce this volume in the innovative *Unbeaten Tracks* series.

Of all instruments, the organ is surrounded by a wide and complex history, and its repertoire is perhaps the oldest and largest. A vast amount of its literature has ecclesiastical associations, and much of the music was composed by organists with a clear liturgical function in mind. In this volume however, the opportunity has been taken to invite composers who are non-organists to contribute and to provide pieces which are entirely abstract in nature – in other words, which are not based on Gregorian or chorale melodies and are not specifically liturgical in inspiration.

Thus the collection encompasses a kaleidoscopic mix of pieces and styles. These include two celebratory, occasional works from Roxanna Panufnik and Graham Fitkin; Diana Burrell and David Matthews have provided pieces of fastidious, quiet intensity; interpretative and technical skill is required to realize the raw energy of Errollyn Wallen's fearsome *Tiger* and Huw Watkins' dynamic *Fanfare*; Judith Bingham provides poetic and lyrical beauty in *St. Bride, assisted by angels*; and the jazz and rock feel of David Bedford's *Carillon* provides further contrast.

Most works can be played on two-manual instruments – given that every organ is in its own way unique, registration markings have been avoided, allowing full scope for imaginative and colourful interpretation. I hope that many organists will take pleasure in exploring and performing this characterful and enjoyable selection of pieces.

John Scott, St. Paul's Cathedral, March 2001

VORWORT

Für mich ist es eine besondere Freude, mit diesem Band in der innovativen Reihe *Unbeaten Tracks* an der Zusammenarbeit von Faber und The Royal College of Organists beteiligt gewesen zu sein.

Die Orgel ist mehr als jedes andere Instrument in einem vielschichtigen und umfassenden historischen Kontext zu sehen. Folgerichtig gehört das Repertoire für Orgel vielleicht zum ältesten und umfangreichsten überhaupt. Die Orgelliteratur ist größtenteils eng mit kirchlichen Aufgabenstellungen verbunden, und viele Orgelwerke entstammen der Feder von Organisten, die ihre Kompositionen für bestimmte liturgische Anlässe schrieben. Für die vorliegende Ausgabe wurden jedoch ausdrücklich Komponisten um Beiträge gebeten, die selbst nicht als Organisten aktiv sind. Eine weitere Vorgabe war zudem die ausdrückliche Bitte nach Kompositionen, die weder auf gregorianischen Melodien oder Choralweisen basieren noch auf besondere liturgische Anlässe zugeschnitten sind.

Die vorliegende Sammlung enthält so eine bunte Mischung von Stücken und Stilrichtungen, darunter zwei feierliche Werke für besondere Anlässe von Roxanna Panufnik und Graham Fitkin. Diana Burrell und David Matthews haben anspruchsvolle Kompositionen von großer Intensität beigesteuert. Zur Ausführung von Errollyn Wallens furchterregendem *Tiger* und Huw Watkins' lebhafter *Fanfare* bedarf es besonderer technischer und interpretatorischer Fähigkeiten. Judith Bingham überzeugt in ihrem Werk *St. Bride, assisted by angels* durch besondere Poesie und Klangschönheit; und einen weiteren Kontrast bedeutet nicht zuletzt David Bedfords Komposition *Carillon* mit ihren Anklängen an Jazz und Rock.

Die meisten Werke lassen sich auf Instrumenten mit zwei Manualen spielen. Da jede Orgel auf ihre Weise ein Unikat ist, wurde bewußt auf Hinweise zur Registrierung verzichtet, um so eine farbige und einfallsreiche Interpretation nicht zu behindern. Ich hoffe, daß viele Organisten an der bunten und reizvollen Sammlung Freude haben werden.

John Scott, St. Paul's Cathedral, März 2001

COMPOSER BIOPICS

All contributing composers were asked to give their own personal responses to the following questions; of course their answers can only reflect their views now and will be ever-changing:

Date and Place of Birth
Musical works that have most inspired you
Individuals who have most inspired you
What your piece means to you
A quote that you feel best describes your music in general
Your two favourite books

ERLÄUTERUNGEN DER KOMPONISTEN

Alle im Band vertretenen Komponisten wurden gebeten, auf die folgenden Fragen eine persönliche Antwort zu finden. Ihre schriftlichen Äußerungen sind selbstverständlich Ausdruck ihres momentanen Urteils und permanentem Wechsel unterworfen.

Datum und Ort Ihrer Geburt
Musikstücke, die Sie am meisten geprägt haben
Persönlichkeiten, die Sie am stärksten geprägt haben
Was bedeutet Ihnen Ihr Stück
Welches Zitat beschreibt Ihre Musik ganz allgemein am besten
Ihre beiden Lieblingsbücher

DAVID BEDFORD

Date and Place of Birth	4.8.37 London
Inspiring musical works	*B minor Mass*, Johann Sebastian Bach; *Marriage of Figaro*, Wolfgang Amadeus Mozart; *Mass of Life*, Frederick Delius; *Pet Sounds*, Beach Boys
Inspiring individuals	My wife, Allison *Meine Frau Allison*
What your piece means to you	I've only ever written 2 organ pieces prior to this, so it's a great and fascinating challenge — organ playing is an art that *must* be kept alive. My piece takes the form of a homage, on a much smaller scale, to the gestures of the French romantic organ writers such as Vierne, Dupré, Duruflé, Widor or Boëllman. The main theme is inspired by the last movement of Vierne's 1st Symphony, but with alternating bars of $4/4$ and $7/8$. Later the typical gestures become subverted by uncharacteristic harmonies and a slow, discordant central section with distorted reminiscences of the main theme. At the end, the theme returns, and the piece ends with the typical grandiose ending of this genre. *Ich habe für Orgel vor diesem Werk überhaupt erst zwei Stücke geschrieben, so daß das Stück für mich eine besondere und faszinierende Herausforderung bedeutete — das Orgelspiel ist eine Kunst, die unbedingt am Leben gehalten werden muß. Mein Werk ist eine Hommage — allerdings in kleinerem Rahmen — an die große Geste französischer romantischer Orgelkomponisten wie Vierne,*

Dupré, Duruflé, Widor oder Boëllman. Das Hauptthema ist inspieriert vom letzten Satz der ersten Symphonie von Vierne, allerdings im Wechsel von $4/4$- und $7/8$-Takt. Im weiteren Verlauf werden die typischen Eigenheiten des Werks durch wenig charaktische Harmonien und einen langsamen, disharmonischen Mittelteil mit verzerrten Reminiszenzen an das Hauptthema unterlaufen. Zum Schluß kehrt das Thema wieder, und das Stück endet mit dem für dieses Genre typischen grandiosen Schluß.

A quote	'One of the most creatively alert and endearing figures in modern British music … he brings to everything he does a refreshingly direct, independent, vitally inquisitive spirit' (Robert Maycock, *The Guardian*) *„Einer der auf kreativste Weise wachen und liebenswerten Figuren der zeitgenössischen englischen Musik … alles zeugt bei ihm von einem erfrischend direkten, unabhängigen und kraftvollen, neugierigen Geist"* (Robert Maycock, The Guardian)
Two favourite books	*The Decline and Fall of the Roman Empire*, Edward Gibbon *Journal of Albion Moonlight*, Kenneth Patchen

JUDITH BINGHAM

Date and Place of Birth	21.6.52 Nottingham
Inspiring musical works	Symphony No.8, Gustav Mahler; *Les Troyens*, Hector Berlioz; *Credo*, Nicolas Gombert; *Franscesca da Rimini*, Pyotr Ilyich Tchaikovsky; *Trauer Ode*, Johann Sebastian Bach; *My Iron Lung*, Radiohead
Inspiring individuals	Hans Keller, Hector Berlioz, Percy Bysshe Shelley, Dmitri Shostakovich, Roger Norrington
What your piece means to you	I was writing at the end of a difficult, unhappy time in my life and wanted to write about Rebirth: St. Bride is the Celtic goddess Brigit reborn, and in legend she visits the Nativity where time itself is reborn. *Ich komponierte [das Stück] am Schluß einer schwierigen, unglücklichen Zeit in meinem Leben und wollte über die Erfahrung der Wiedergeburt schreiben: St. Bride ist die wiedergeborene keltische Göttin Brigit. Der Legende nach besucht sie den Ort der Christgeburt, wo die Zeit selbst wiedergeboren wird.*
A quote	'A dark subtle poetry, accessing the spiritual through a ravishing soundscape' *„Eine dunkle, empfindsame Sprache, die sich Spirituellem durch herrliche Klänge nähert"*
Two favourite books	*Landscape and Memory*, Simon Schama *Great Expectations*, Charles Dickens

GRAHAM FITKIN

Date and Place of Birth	19.04.63 Cornwall
Inspiring musical works	*De Materie*, Louis Andriessen; *Reprazent*, Roni Size
Inspiring individuals	Alfred Hitchcock; Patrick Caulfield
What your piece means to you	Camp, kitsch, majestic and largely in C *Kitsch, großartig und vorwiegend in C-dur*
A quote	'God knows why I like it' *„Keine Ahnung, warum ich das mag"*
Two favourite books	*White Noise*, Don DeLillo *The Prince*, Niccolo Machiavelli

DIANA BURRELL

Date and Place of Birth	25.10.48 Norwich
Inspiring musical works	*The Midsummer Marriage*, Michael Tippett; *Vespers*, Claudio Monteverdi; everything by Carl Nielsen, especially Symphony No.4
Inspiring individuals	My husband Richard, and all the rest of my lovely family and friends *Mein Mann Richard, meine ganze wunderbare Familie und alle Freunde*
What your piece means to you	In writing for the organ, a composer must bravely relinquish final control of colour and sound to the performer. Every instrument sounds so different and I love the unpredictability. *Der Komponist muß bei einem Werk für Orgel die letzte Entscheidung über Klang und Farbe vertrauensvoll dem Interpreten überlassen. Jedes Instrument klingt anders; ich liebe dieses Element des Unvorhersehbaren.*
A quote	'… the strongest and strangest music I've heard in years' (Chris Dench, *Soundscapes*) *„… die stärkste und merkwürdigste Musik seit langem"* (Chris Dench, Soundscapes)
Two favourite books	*The Bone People*, Keri Hulme *The Book of Laughter and Forgetting*, Milan Kundera

DAVID MATTHEWS

Date and Place of Birth	9.3.43 London
Inspiring musical works	*Vespers*, Claudio Monteverdi; String Quartet in C sharp minor, Op.131, Ludwig van Beethoven; *Tapiola*, Jean Sibelius; *Jack the Bear*, Duke Ellington
Inspiring individuals	Michael Tippett; Peter Sculthorpe
What your piece means to you	It's the first time I've tried to write for organ – I was rather terrified! But I was seduced by its sensuousness and its power. *Dieses ist mein erster Versuch mit einem Werk für Orgel – es war ein ziemliches Abenteuer! Aber ich ließ mich einfangen von der Klangfülle und Klanggewalt des Instruments.*
A quote	'Full of dark poetry and haunted vistas' *„Voll dunkler Poesie und gespenstischer Anklänge"*
Two favourite books	*Landscape and Memory*, Simon Schama *The Lord of the Rings*, J.R.R.Tolkien

ROXANNA PANUFNIK

Date and Place of Birth	24.4.68 London
Inspiring musical works	*Requiem*, Gabriel Fauré; Piano Concerto No.2, Maurice Ravel; *Stabat mater*, Karol Szymanowski; *Turangalîla-symphonie*, Olivier Messiaen
Inspiring individuals	Sister Raphael; Hans Werner Henze; Melanie Daiken; Vikram Seth; George Herbert
What your piece means to you	Faber asked me to write this piece round about the same time I heard that my cousin Samantha had got engaged — she and her husband Stuart came back down the aisle to this piece and so now, whenever I hear it, I can see their ecstatic faces! *Faber gab dieses Stück etwa zu der Zeit in Auftrag, als ich von der Verlobung meiner Kusine Samantha erfuhre — sie und ihr Mann schritten zu dieser Musik als Paar durch die Kirche, so daß mir bei jedem erneuten Hören dieser Musik ihre verklärten Gesichter vor Augen sind!*
A quote	'…a gifted young composer with a fast-growing reputation for heart, spunk and individuality … distinctive in voice, serious, bold and appealing' (Fiona Maddocks, *The Observer*) *„Eine begabte junge Komponistin mit einer stetig wachsenden Reputation für ihre gefühlvolle, lebhafte und individuelle Tonsprache … eine klar erkennbare eigene Stimme, ernst, mutig und ansprechend!"* (Fiona Maddocks, The Observer*)*
Two favourite books	*David Copperfield*, Charles Dickens *Music and Silence*, Rose Tremain

ERROLLYN WALLEN

Date and Place of Birth	10.4.58 Belize
Inspiring musical works	Symphony No.7, Beethoven; *Goldberg Variations*, J.S.Bach
Inspiring individuals	J.S.Bach; Ella Fitzgerald; Howard Hodgkin; various imaginary individuals *Verschiedene imaginäre Persönlichkeiten*
What your piece means to you	This piece is about life — the rage of its raw energy. It is also about remembering my friend, the poet Veronica Rospigliosi, who died on Christmas Day 1999. As she lay dying, she said, 'I am thinking about the shape of a tiger'. That is how I got the idea for the piece. *Dieses Stück handelt vom Leben — von der Heftigkeit seiner ungezügelten Energie. Es handelt auch von der Erinnerung an meine Freundin, die Dichterin Veronica Rospigliosi, die an Weihnachten 1999 starb. Als sie im Sterben lag, sagte sie: „Ich denke an die Gestalt eines Tigers". So bekam ich die Idee zu diesem Stück.*
A quote	'Bright, funky, irreducible' (Jez Nelson, *What's On Magazine*) *„Klug, witzig, nicht weiter zu vereinfachen"* (Jez Nelson, What's On Magazine*)*
Two favourite books	*Nostromo*, Joseph Conrad The A-Z of London

HUW WATKINS

Date and Place of Birth	13.7.76 Pontypool, Wales
Inspiring musical works	Piano Quartets in G minor and E♭ major, Wolfgang Amadeus Mozart; *Curlew River*, Benjamin Britten; Duo for Violin and piano, Elliott Carter; Two songs, Op.91, for contralto, viola and piano, Johannes Brahms
Inspiring individuals	Musically and compositionally: Julian Anderson *Musikalisch und kompositorisch: Julian Anderson*
What your piece means to you	My organ piece is meant to be an exuberant and colourful fanfare, which ends unashamedly in C major. *Mein Orgelstück ist eine übermütige und farbenreiche Fanfare, die ganz schamlos in C-dur endet.*
A quote	'[The nineties was a period in which] a young talent such as Huw Watkins, emerging from an entirely classical background, could still engage his listeners, not out of some cute mix of current styles, but through the cogency of his compositional invention' (Bayon Northcott, *The Independent*) *„[Die neunziger Jahre waren eine Zeit,] in der ein junges Talent wie Huw Watkins, der von der Klassik her kam, seine Zuhörer immer noch fesseln konnte, und zwar nicht durch eine geschickte Mischung aktueller Stilrichtungen, sondern durch die Überzeugungskraft seiner kompositorischen Erfindung"* (Bayon Northcott, The Independent*)*
Two favourite books	*The Magus*, John Fowles *If on a Winter's Night a Traveller*, Italo Calvino

Fanfare

Huw Watkins

Fragment I

Diana Burrell

Gentle, distant, but with colour ♩ = *c*.60

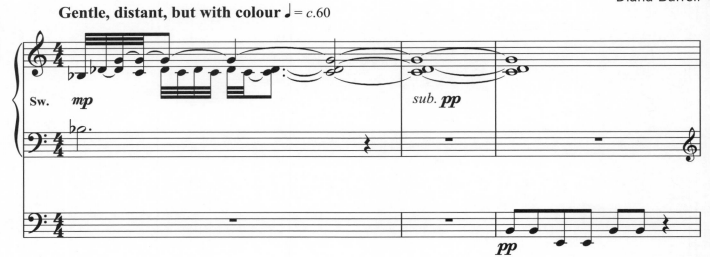

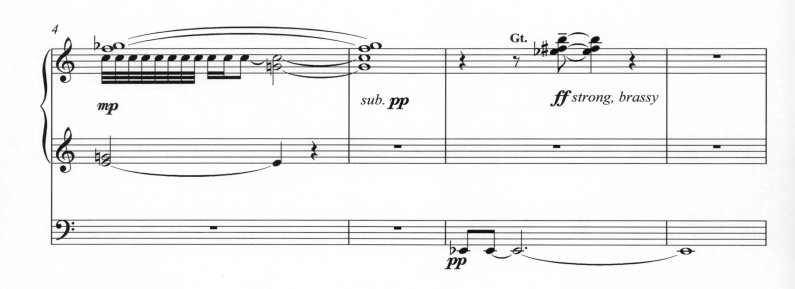

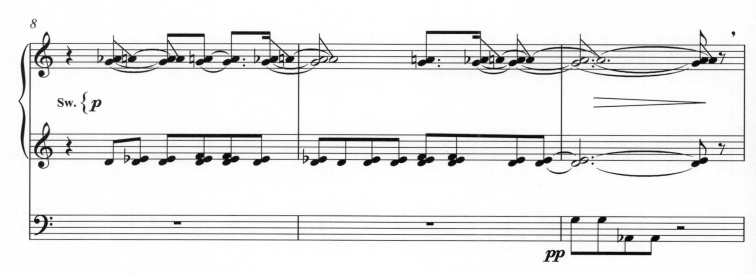

May 2000

Fragment II

Light and elusive, long lines ♩ = *c.*100

Diana Burrell

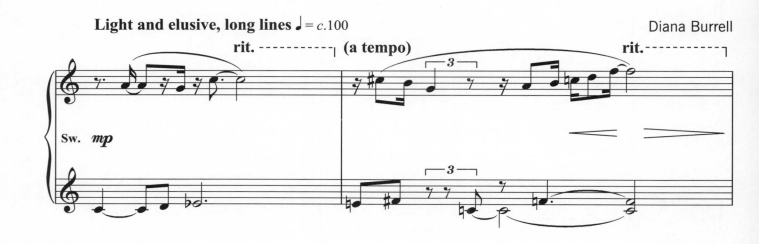

13

Nov. 2000

to Mantha and Stu on their wedding day

Bridal Train

Roxanna Panufnik

16

* on 2 manuals if possible/desired

Invocation

David Matthews

in memoriam Veronica Rospigliosi

dedicated to John and Sally Butt

Tiger

Errollyn Wallen

senza rit.

+ 32'

Cambridge, June 2000

for Eleanor and Tom

Wedding

Graham Fitkin

St. Bride, assisted by angels

A strange sun rising on a barely swelling sea . . .

Judith Bingham

Clouds veil the sky's mystery . . .

The poetry that partly replaces expression marks in the score is not meant to be reproduced separately but is for the eyes of the performer only.

Night rises from his cold dark bed . . .

Tempo I Backwards in time to the beginnings of her faith she goes . . .   to the Nativity, where God made

time begin anew.   A memory of past time,

at once sweet and sad . . .

full of longing, regret . . .

. . . forgiveness . . .

. . . and love.

mp very ethereal

poco rall.

London, August 2000

Carillon

David Bedford

44

Faber New Choral Works

General Editor: Simon Halsey

Faber New Choral Works introduces a wealth of new or recently written
choral music to choirs in search of fresh repertoire.
The series draws in a rich diversity of living composers and includes both lighter
and more challenging contemporary works, offering a thrilling array of varied styles.

Faber New Choral Works

Thomas Adès	The Fayrfax Carol	ISBN 0-571-51835-4
Thomas Adès	January Writ	ISBN 0-571-52036-7
Jonathan Dove	Seek Him that Maketh the Seven Stars	ISBN 0-571-51828-1
Jonathan Dove	Into Thy Hands	ISBN 0-571-51829-X
Jonathan Dove	Ecce Beatam Lucem	ISBN 0-571-51846-X
Jonathan Dove	Wellcome, all Wonders in One Sight!	ISBN 0-571-51905-9
Howard Goodall	In Memoriam Anne Frank	ISBN 0-571-51931-8
Howard Goodall	The Lord is my shepherd (Psalm 23)	ISBN 0-571-52048-0
Howard Goodall	Love divine (SSAA)	ISBN 0-571-52043-X
Howard Goodall	Love divine (SATB)	ISBN 0-571-52044-8
Howard Goodall	The Marlborough Canticles: Magnificat & Nunc dimittis	ISBN 0-571-51877-X
Francis Grier	Alleluia! I Bring You News of Great Joy	ISBN 0-571-51847-8
Francis Grier	Two Advent Responsories – I Look from Afar/Judah and Jerusalem: Fear Not	ISBN 0-571-51848-6
Wayne Marshall	Magnificat & Nunc dimittis in C	ISBN 0-571-52073-1
Philip Moore	Lo! God is here!	ISBN 0-571-52068-5
Antony Pitts	Adoro te	ISBN 0-571-52083-9
Antony Pitts	Libera Me/Lamentations 5	ISBN 0-571-51830-3
Peter Sculthorpe	Morning Song for the Christ Child/The Birthday of thy King	ISBN 0-571-52069-3
Michael Zev Gordon	And I Will Betroth You	ISBN 0-571-51856-7

A CD of thirteen of the Faber New Choral Works is available direct from Faber Music Ltd
Schola Cantorum of Oxford / Mark Shepherd   ISBN 0-571-51971-7

Faber Music Ltd, Burnt Mill, Elizabeth Way, Harlow CM20 2HX
Tel: +44 (0)1279 82 89 82   Fax: +44 (0)1279 82 89 83
sales@fabermusic.com   www.fabermusic.com

FABER **ƒƒ** MUSIC